GET SPORTY

Swimming

Edward Way

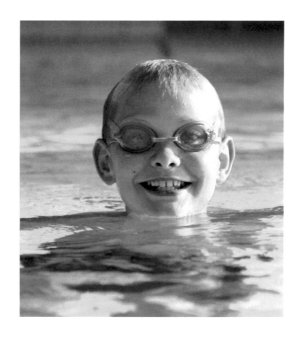

WAYLAND

First published in 2010 by Wayland

Copyright © Wayland 2010

Wayland
338 Euston Road
London NW1 3BH

Wayland Australia
Level 17/207 Kent Street
Sydney NSW 2000

Editor: Nicola Edwards
Designer: www.rawshock.co.uk

British Library Cataloguing in
Publication Data

Way, Edward
 Swimming. -- (Get sporty)
 1. Swimming--Juvenile literature.
 I. Title II. Series
 797.2'1-dc22

ISBN: 978 0 7502 6111 1

Picture acknowledgements:
Photographs by Clive Gifford except
for p4 (l) iStockphoto; p5 (b) LIU JIN/
AFP/Getty Images; p6 (l, r, t) Michael
Wicks, (b) iStockphoto; p7 (all)
Michael Wicks; p8 iStockphoto; p9
(tl) iStockphoto, (tr, bl) Michael Wicks;
pp10, 11 (all) Michael Wicks; p12 (t)
iStockphoto, (b) Michael Wicks; p13
(l) Michael Wicks, (r) Clive Rose/Getty
Images; pp14-16 (all) Michael Wicks;
p17 (t) Donald Miralle/Getty Images;
(b) iStockphoto; p19 All Michael
Wicks except (b) GERARD JULIEN/
AFP/Getty Images; pp20-21, p22 (b)
Shutterstock; pp23-26 (all) Michael
Wicks; p25 (b) Ryan Pierse/Getty
Images; p27 (l, r) Michael Wicks, (b)
Mike Powell/Getty Images; p28 (tr, bl,
br), p29 (tl, tr) Michael Wicks; p29 (bl)
iStockphoto, (br) JEAN-CHRISTOPHE
VERHAEGEN/AFP/Getty Images.
The author and publisher would
like to thank Mitchell Cameron and
Ben Cameron for their help with the
photographs for this book.
Printed in China.

Wayland is a division of Hachette
Children's Books, an Hachette UK
company.
www.hachette.co.uk

CONTENTS

LEARN TO SWIM

As well as being great fun, swimming is a skill you can use throughout your life. It is also an exciting sport in which swimmers compete to be the fastest.

FUN AND EXERCISE

Many people swim for fun on holiday and at their local pool. Swimming is also great exercise, which is why athletes in other sports often swim as part of their training. Swimming races are held over a range of distances. At the Olympics, the shortest race is 50 metres long. The longest is held in open water and is an incredible 10,000 metres long!

1 These two brothers are on holiday and have challenged each other to a swimming race. They hold onto the edge of the pool, called the pool wall. At the start of the race, they push off the wall and get their faces in the water.

TOP TIP You may have learned to swim at your local pool. Many pools also have extra lessons for boys and girls who can already swim. These lessons will help you improve their skills.

2 The boys try to swim as fast and as smoothly as possible. They are using a swimming stroke called the front crawl.

3 Swimmers aim to time their surge at the finish of the race to touch the pool wall first with their hand.

4 Winning even a fun race amongst friends can be great fun. If you don't win, always congratulate the winner. You can work hard on your swimming technique to beat them next time.

PRO PLAY

Eleanor Simmonds took up swimming at the age of five, after she was inspired by watching Nyree Lewis win a gold medal at the 2004 Paralympics in Athens, Greece. Here, Simmonds has just won her 400 metres race at the 2008 Paralympics in Beijing, China. Simmonds became the youngest ever Paralympic gold medallist. She was just 13 years old.

GET STARTED

You do not need a lot of equipment to take part in swimming. A good swimsuit and pair of goggles are enough to get you started.

SWIMMING KIT

There are other things you can pack in your swim bag including a towel and shampoo or shower gel. You should always take a shower before entering a pool and after your swim. A bottle of water or juice is good to take with you because swimming can be a real workout and make you thirsty.

If you have long hair, tuck it away underneath a stretchy swimcap. This stops your hair getting in your face.

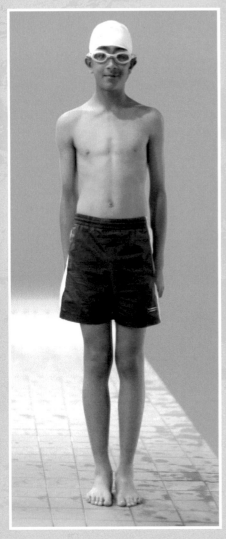

Boys may wear long swimming shorts when on holiday, but for swimming fast, a pair of trunks is best.

A good swimsuit for girls is made of stretchy material so it fits closely.

Wearing goggles allows you to see where you are going when you are swimming underwater. Always put the goggles on your face first, then stretch the band around your head.

DIFFERENT STROKES

There are four main strokes used in swimming races.

The most popular swimming stroke is front crawl. Swimmers lie on their front with their arms reaching into the water in front of them.

To swim the breaststroke, a swimmer's arms and legs stay in the water at all times. The head rises to take a breath.

The one stroke you swim on your back is called back crawl. Swimmers kick their feet and swing their arms up through the air and then down through the water.

To perform the butterfly, both arms leave the water and sweep through the air at the same time.

THE POOL AND RULES

Swimming pools for serious races are rectangle-shaped and come in two types. Short course pools are 25 metres long. Long course pools are 50 metres in length.

These swimmers are competing in a race at a swimming meet or gala. Each swims down a narrow corridor of the pool called a lane. Any swimmer who changes lanes will be disqualified and out of the race.

TOP TIP

Follow these swimming Dos and Don'ts:
- NEVER dive in the shallow end.
- Never run around the edge of the pool. It is often slippery and if you fall onto the hard surface you could hurt yourself badly.
- Always obey a lifeguard or swimming teacher's instructions.
- Keep looking where you are going as you swim.

The pool is where you will train, improve your swimming skills and, when you're ready, take part in races. Pools for swimming club sessions or for races are usually split into lanes so that individuals can swim at their own speed. There is usually a large clock on the wall, so swimmers can time their swims.

The pool is divided into separate lanes by long strings of floats. Always stay in your lane. If you have to cross lanes, make sure the way is clear.

Starting blocks are fitted to one end of many pools. Butterfly, breaststroke and front crawl swimmers start races by standing on the blocks and diving in.

A line of flags hangs above each end of the pool, five metres from the pool's edge. This is for back crawl swimmers to see how far they are away from the pool wall.

Always climb in and out of a pool using the pool steps. Grip the rungs with both hands and ease yourself in and out of the water.

SWIM FRONT CRAWL

The front crawl is fastest stroke. This is why swimmers use it in freestyle races when they are allowed to choose any stroke.

TECHNIQUE

To swim front crawl you have to stay flat and narrow in the water. Your arms and legs move all the time. The arms work alternately; as one arm strokes through the water the other moves through the air.

1 Slide your left arm into the water ahead of you. Your hand should slice through the water with your elbow high.

2 Sweep your arm down and back through the water strongly. Your other arm leaves the water, elbow first.

3 Keeping your fingers together, your left arm sweeps back and towards the centre of your body...

4 ...All the way to your thigh. At the same time your right hand, fingers together, passes your head and enters the water in front of you.

5 Your left arm leaves the water, elbow first. It will travel low over the water and enter the water ahead of your head.

Viewed from the front, you can see how narrow the movement of the arms is compared with the butterfly or breaststroke. Both arms pass close by the body.

TOP TIPS

Try to keep your body in a straight line with your hips and legs directly behind you. Imagine you are swimming through a narrow tube without touching the sides.

Stay as flat as possible. This helps you cut through the water.

Your face should be in the water but the top of your head should be above it.

Keep your hips high and just underneath the water's surface.

IMPROVE YOUR FRONT CRAWL

To swim the front crawl well, you have to time your arm and leg movements carefully. You need to control the speed of your strokes and get a good rhythm going.

THE LEG KICK

The leg kick in the front crawl starts from the thigh. You bend your knee only slightly as you beat each leg up and down. Your feet should be stretched back at the ankles with your toes pointing back and slightly inwards.

You can practise the leg kick by using a float called a kickboard that you hold in your hands. Keep your face in the water as you kick.

One of the most common mistakes is to only kick your lower leg by bending your knee too much. This sends your foot and lower leg out of the water. It creates a big splash and wastes much of the power of your kick.

BREATHING

You breathe by turning your head to the side as the arm on that side leaves the water. Take a good breath. Then, turn your head back so that your face returns to the water.

Keep your shoulders level with your head. Part of your face should stay in the water all the time even when you are breathing.

TOP TIPS

Many new swimmers stop kicking their legs when they try to breathe. Keep kicking at all times. You can practise kicking and breathing by holding the edge of the pool and stretching your body out.

A streamlined shape helps you travel through the water faster. Try to keep your eyes looking ahead when your face is in the water.

PRO PLAY

This underwater picture shows the leg kick used by front crawl swimmers in a race. Nearest to the camera is 400-m and 800-m champion Rebecca Adlington. Notice how her legs stay under the water all the time as she kicks.

SWIM BACK CRAWL

Back crawl is the only stroke you swim on your back. Your legs kick all the time as first one arm then the other sweeps through the water then travels high through the air.

TECHNIQUE

When you swim the back crawl, your body lies flat and narrow in the water. Your head faces the ceiling with your eyes looking up and backwards a little. Your hips stay high near the surface of the water. This helps keep your legs, which are stretched out, a little lower in the water.

1 As one of your arms travels through the air, turn your wrist so that your palm faces outwards.

2 Slide your arm into the water with your hand entering little finger first. Your arm sweeps out and down, pushing against the water.

3 Your elbow bends as you push your arm down and back towards your feet.

4 Your hand leaves the water thumb first. It will travel high and straight through the air to start another stroke.

 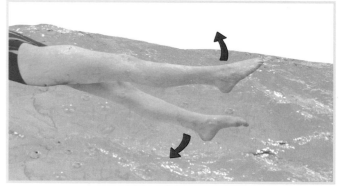

Keep your legs long and straight as you kick from your hips. One leg goes down as the other leg goes up.

Your feet can just break the water's surface at the top of their kick. But keep your ankles a little loose and make sure your legs pass by each other closely.

TOP TIPS Keep your hips high. Don't sit in the water with your bottom dropping down deep.

Your arm should travel narrowly past your body through the air to land in the water ahead of you.

As you make the arm movements, your body should roll a little from side to side. Try to keep your head as flat in the water as possible.

Practise hard to build a smooth rhythm to your arm and leg movements. Breathe in as one arm enters the water and out as the other arm enters.

SWIM BREASTSTROKE

Breaststroke is one of the most popular swimming strokes. You can learn the unusual arm and leg movements separately and then put them together.

IN OR OUT

Breaststroke can be swum with your head above the water all the time. But it is a much faster and smoother stroke if you keep your face in the water, only lifting it to breathe.

1 Start with your hands together and your arms out in front of you as you glide forward.

2 Point your palms outwards and sweep your arms out and slightly down.

3 Your elbows stay high as your arms continue to sweep. Just before they reach your shoulders, they start to sweep down and in so that they head underneath your chin.

4 Your palms face each other as your hands sweep under your chin. Your head rises with your arms and your legs start to bend to perform the kick (see page 18).

5 Your arms start to stretch forwards with the palms turned to face down. You will get into the glide position (stage 1) before starting another set of arm movements.

TOP TIP Your two arms should mirror the movement of each other. Make sure they move through the stroke at the same time and with the same speed and power.

When you glide, keep your face in the water but with your eyes looking ahead. Your arms are stretched out pressing gently against your ears.

Your hands and arms should stay underneath the water at all times. Keep your body as flat in the water as possible.

A good breaststroke action gives you time to breathe. As your hands move inwards on their way to getting underneath your chin, your shoulders and head rises. Take a breath then before your head sinks back under the water.

PRO PLAY

American champion swimmer Michael Phelps surges forward in a breaststroke race as his arms begin to move in front of him. In 2008 in Beijing, China, Phelps made history by becoming the first person to win eight gold medals at a single Olympic Games.

MORE ABOUT BREASTSTROKE

The leg action takes time to get right. Make sure your head, shoulders and body are level. This helps keep both legs level throughout the kick. Also, remember to keep your legs under the water throughout the leg movement.

THE LEG KICK

1 You bend your knees and bring the heels of your feet up to your bottom. The soles of your feet point up.

2 Your feet are turned outwards as you kick round and back with plenty of power.

3 Your leg kick continues until your legs are out wide and are fully stretched.

4 Your legs sweep together to perform the glide stage. Then, you start to bend your legs at the knee again to begin the next leg kick.

Learning to time the movements of your arms and legs together is a key to breaststroke success. To help you perfect your technique, think pull-kick-glide.

Pull with the arms, kick with the legs and then glide along, before starting the next stroke with another pull of the arms. As your arms sweep under your chin, take a breath, bend your knees and start the leg movement.

TOP TIPS

The breaststroke may seem unusual at first but lots of practice will help make it feel more natural. You can practise in the shallow end of a pool: push off from the wall, get into a glide position and then try to perform one arm and leg stroke.

You can practise timing the breaststroke leg kick by holding a kickboard ahead of you with your hands or gripping the edge of the pool wall.

PRO PLAY

Here you can see how a top swimmer, Britain's James Gibson, times his leg and arm movements. His legs thrust backwards powerfully with his feet turned out as his arms begin to stretch out in front of him.

SWIM BUTTERFLY

The butterfly is the most difficult stroke to perfect and is usually the last one you will learn. It is exciting even if it will leave you tired – it's hard to swim butterfly for more than short distances.

TECHNIQUE

To swim butterfly your body surges and plunges through the water as your arms and legs move together. Your legs perform a complete kick up and down, called the dolphin kick, for every complete stroke of your arms.

1 Put your hands in the water in front of your shoulders. Your palms should face outwards.

2 Your arms sweep downwards and back towards your feet. Your elbows stay higher than your hands.

3 Your arms continue to sweep back but move inwards. As your arms sweep back, your hips and head start to rise.

4 Your arms leave the water, elbows first. Your head continues to rise, lifting your chin out of the water. Now is the time when you can take a breath.

5 From the side you can see how your shoulders and head should come out of the water just as your arms leave the water as well. As the arms rise and move forward, your head sinks back down, face into the water.

Your arms sweep wide but low over the water. They are flung forwards so they will enter the water shoulder-width apart to begin another stroke.

THE DOLPHIN KICK

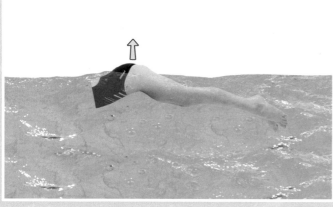

1 As your legs rise, lift your bottom but stay under the water. Both your legs should move together at the same time like a wave.

2 Your legs beat upwards so that your toes break the surface of the water.

3 The tops of your feet press down on the water as your lower legs whip downwards with your knees bending.

4 Your legs carry on kicking down until they are straight and your knees are no longer bent. Your bottom will start to rise to begin the kick again.

FAST STARTS

In a swimming race, you need a fast start. Breaststroke, front crawl and butterfly races start with a grab dive from the starting blocks. Back crawl races start with the swimmers already in the water.

LEARNING TO DIVE

If you cannot dive yet, you can still have fun races with friends with each of you starting in the water, holding the pool wall.

You can learn to dive in stages. This swimmer is performing a crouch dive, leaning forward and entering the pool with his arms first.

READY, SET, GO!

In all races, like the one shown here, you have to wait for the starter's signal. This can be a blast on a whistle, a starting gun firing or a shout of "Go!". If you start to dive or swim before the starting signal, you have made a false start. In major competitions, any swimmer who makes a false start is sent out of the race. The race is then restarted.

TOP TIP Once in the water, make yourself as narrow as possible as you glide underwater. This will mean you will lose less speed before you come to the surface and start swimming.

BACK CRAWL START

1 Hold the rail and pull yourself into a coiled position. At the starting signal, pull up with your arms.

2 Push hard with your feet and throw your arms backwards as fast as you can.

3 Your hands come together with your head between your arms as you glide away.

THE GRAB DIVE

1 Stand on your starting block with your hands and toes gripping the front edge. Look down at the water ahead of you.

2 As the race starts you pull your body forward, bend your knees and swing your arms forwards.

3 Straighten your legs and push hard off the blocks. As you dive up and out your arms come together, fingers pointing at the water.

4 Lift your hips to raise your legs up. With your hands punch a hole in the water through which the rest of your body will follow.

LET'S RACE!

There are several different types of swimming race. There are races for all four of the different strokes. Some are sprints like the 25, 50 and 100 metres. Others are longer races over 200m or more.

RELAY RACING

Teams of four swimmers swim exciting relay races. Each competitor swims the same distance. One swimmer must complete their swim and touch the pool wall before the next swimmer can leave the starting blocks.

1 As her team-mate approaches, the next swimmer in a relay team is ready to start. She swings her arms back and leans forward with her knees bent.

2 She watches her team-mate touch the wall then straight away swings her arms forward and dives into the water.

3 Her legs have pushed strongly off the blocks and her hands come together in front of her body.

4 Her legs and arms are together as her hands enter the water. She will try to glide away and start swimming quickly.

MEDLEYS

Medleys are races in which competitors swim all four strokes. Team medleys are relay races in which each swimmer in a team swims a different stroke.

In an individual medley race each competitor swims butterfly, followed by back crawl, then breaststroke before swimming front crawl to the finish. You have to be really good at all four strokes to take part in these races.

When you are taking part in a relay race, you also need to know how to change from one stroke to another.

TOP TIP

In relays and all races, timing your finish is really important. Try to touch the wall with your fingers stretched out.

1 This swimmer has finished swimming butterfly and touches the wall with both hands. She now pulls her knees up beneath her body.

2 She leans back and pushes off with both legs. Her arms travel through the air. She will glide away and then start to swim the back crawl.

PRO PLAY

Stephanie Rice performs the breaststroke part of the 200m individual medley race at the 2010 Australian Championships. Rice won this competition to go with her three wins at the 2008 Olympics — one in a relay and two in individual medley events.

MAKE A TURN

In many swimming races competitors have to swim more than one length of the pool. This means that swimmers have to learn how to make special turns to lose as little time as possible.

THE TUMBLE TURN

Swimmers use a tumble turn when they are swimming the front crawl. It is like a forward somersault in the water with the swimmer's feet reaching the wall. With knees bent, the legs push off the wall.

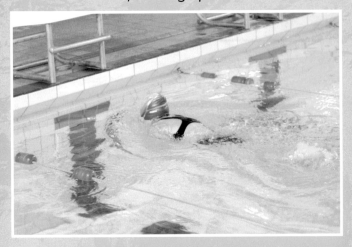

1 The swimmer swims up to the pool wall at her regular speed. The rules of racing allow her to touch the wall with her feet but not with her hands.

2 She dips her chin to her chest, bends at the hips and drives her head down into the water. Her legs and feet start to rise.

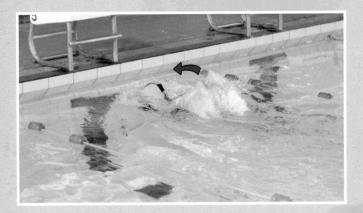

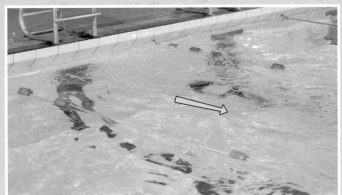

3 The swimmer turns upside-down in the water with her feet coming over and reaching the pool wall.

4 The swimmer pushes off the pool wall. While she is underwater, she twists so that she is on her front with her arms in front of her. She glides away smoothly.

THE BACK CRAWL TURN

As you approach the pool wall, roll over onto your front and perform a tumble turn. The big difference is that you stay on your back and don't roll over like you do with the front crawl turn.

TWO-HANDED TURNING

In butterfly and breaststroke races, you have to touch the wall with both hands as you make your turn, so you need to use a different type of turn.

1 Touch the wall with both hands, bend your knees up close to the wall and turn sideways. Take one hand off the wall.

2 Throw your arm away from the wall and turn your body. Your feet can push off from the pool wall to help you power away.

PRO PLAY

Here, you can see how a good swimmer starts to twist her body during the front crawl turn so that she can glide away on her front.

TOP TIPS Practise your turns by swimming four or five strokes up to a wall then performing a turn. Try to swim at your normal speed as you reach the pool wall.

If your fingers don't reach the wall in a turn, don't swim a whole extra arm stroke. Instead, perform an extra leg kick. Remember to stay streamlined after you make the turn.

MAKING THE TEAM

There's a lot of hard work ahead if you want to improve enough to join a school or club swimming team. But swimming in competitions is very exciting and well worth all the effort.

PRACTISE AND IMPROVE

A major way to improve is to correct the mistakes you make when you swim. One common error is to not kick equally strongly with both legs. As a result, you may find yourself veering off from a straight line down the pool. Another mistake is to try to swim too fast only to run out of steam. Work on swimming at a speed you can keep up for a while.

This front crawl swimmer's arm is travelling far too high in the air. Your arms should stay low to enter the water ahead of the swimmer at the right angle.

Make sure your head doesn't come too far out of the water when you are swimming breaststroke or front crawl.

When you're swimming back crawl try not to let your hips sink down into the water. You can grip a special float called a pool buoy between your thighs to help keep your hips high.

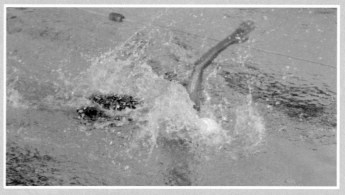

If you make a big splash when you swim it's is a sign that you are not swimming correctly. Your feet should stay under the water and your hands and arms should always enter the water smoothly.

A swimming coach can help you improve greatly by pointing out mistakes you are making and showing you how to swim faster and more smoothly. But it is up to you to work hard to put your coach's suggestions into practice.

Swimmers often build their fitness away from the swimming pool by running or cycling.

Before swimming a race or starting training in the pool, you should stretch all your major muscles. A coach can show you how to do this.

PRO PLAY

These swimmers are practising their dives and turns in a competition swimming pool before a swimming meet takes place. It is a good idea to check out a new pool before you race in it.

GLOSSARY

back crawl
A swimming stroke where the swimmer lies on their back and kicks their legs up and down whilst sweeping each arm overhead and then through the water.

breaststroke
A swimming stroke performed on your front with your arms making circular sweeping movements and your legs kicking with a pushing action.

buoy
A floating object in the water which can be used as a swim training aid.

butterfly
A type of swimming stroke performed face down with your arms sweeping over your head at the same time.

dolphin kick
A type of kick used when swimming the butterfly stroke where the legs kick up and down together.

false start
When one or more of the swimmers leave their starting blocks before the race begins.

freestyle
Races or events which allow you to swim using any stroke you choose. This is usually front crawl as it is the fastest swimming stroke.

front crawl
A powerful swimming stroke where the swimmer swims on their front and makes long sweeping strokes of their arms whilst kicking with their legs.

grab dive
A simple type of dive from the pool edge or on a block, used by many swimmers to enter the water.

kickboard
A floating board swimmers can hold onto as they practise their kicking and body movement in the water.

lane
A narrow corridor in a swimming pool down which a swimmer swims when in a race.

long course
A race or event held in a swimming pool which measures 50m in length.

medley
An event where one swimmer or a team swims separate parts of the race using all four major strokes: backstroke, breaststroke, butterfly and freestyle.

open water race
A race held not in a swimming pool but in a river, lake or sea.

Paralympics
The major sports competition for top athletes with a disability which takes place in the weeks after an Olympic Games.

short course
Races held in swimming pools which measure 25m in length.

starter
The official who begins a race with a signal such as firing a starting pistol.

starting blocks
Raised platforms which swimmers stand on just before beginning breaststroke, butterfly or freestyle races.

streamlined
To form a smooth shape in the water so that you move through it as smoothly and quickly as possible.

tumble turn
An underwater turn at an end of the pool which lets the swimmer push off for the next length with their feet.

RESOURCES

BOOKS

Sporting Skills: Swimming – Clive Gifford, Wayland, 2007.
For slightly older readers, this book uses step by step photography and diagrams to really get into the techniques of swimming strokes and races.

Starting Sport: Swimming – Rebecca Hunter, Franklin Watts, 2008
A fun guide to learning how to swim with lots of pictures.

Training To Succeed: Swimming – Rita Storey, Watts, 2009
This book looks at the lives of a group of teenage swimmers who are hoping to make it in professional swimming.

WEBSITES

http://www.dunedinswimteam.co.uk/swimming_tips.htm
See all the swimming strokes in action in these simple, fun cartoons.

http://news.bbc.co.uk/sport1/hi/other_sports/swimming/default.stm
The BBC swimming webpages have lots of news and features on star swimmers as well as top tips for learning to swim the strokes.

http://www.swimming.org/britishswimming/swimming
The official website of British Swimming has news about swimming events, top swimmers and a history of the sport.

Swimming takes time to learn and improve and there are lots of tips to remember. But there is one tip that is more important than any other – make sure you have fun! Learning to swim and improving your swimming strokes can be done with friends in swimming classes and clubs. So why not round up some of your friends and…Get Sporty!

INDEX

Get Sporty

Contents of titles in the series:

WAYLAND